Kathleen T. McWhorter

INSTRUCTOR'S MANUAL TO ACCOMPANY

EFFICIENT AND FLEXIBLE READING

Instructor's Manual to Accompany

EFFICIENT AND FLEXIBLE READING

Kathleen T. McWhorter

Niagara County Community College

Little, Brown and Company

Boston Toronto

ISBN 0-316-56407-9

5 4 3 2 1

SEM

Published simultaneously in Canada
by Little, Brown & Company (Canada) Limited

Printed in the United States of America

CONTENTS

Chapter 1

BASIC FEATURES OF THE TEXT

The text was written in response to the need for development of efficient and flexible reading skills and provides sufficient opportunity for their practice and application. Many of its basic features are described in the following section.

EMPHASIS ON EFFICIENCY AND FLEXIBILITY

Reading is an integration of learned behaviors, skills, attitudes, and personal resources that results in the understanding, interpretation, and evaluation of printed material, as well as application of its content. As such it is a complex task, influenced simultaneously by numerous factors. By the time they enter college, most students have acquired a foundation of reading skills; they have acquired basic word-recognition skills, phonetic and structural analysis skills, and a functioning level of basic comprehension skills that allow them to understand and recall textual material. However, most college students have not developed the spectrum of skills and abilities that characterize an efficient and flexible reader. They read relatively slowly and have difficulty comprehending and recalling difficult material. They frequently lose concentration and have to reread. Most students have one general approach to reading, characterized by a very narrow range of reading speed. Students seldom adjust their rate deliberately to suit their purpose or the type of material they are reading, and have limited awareness of the interaction between rate and comprehension. The emphasis throughout this text, then, is on the development of reading efficiency and flexibility.

Reading efficiency is a relative term that describes the interaction between reading rate and comprehension to meet the needs of the readers with the least time and effort expended. Efficiency, in a sense, describes a balance between two important variables: rate and comprehension. The balance, in part, hinges on the reader's interest, skills and abilities, background knowledge, and familiarity with the subject.

Reading flexibility can be defined as the ability to adjust both rate and level of comprehension to suit one's purpose, the nature of the reading material, and the reading situation. The concept implies that every reading situation is unique and that both rate and level of comprehension should be adjusted to suit the particular circumstances.

BALANCE BETWEEN RATE THE COMPREHENSION

Many basic reading texts emphasize the development of literal comprehension skills; others, commonly known as speed reading texts, emphasize rate increase. Unlike each of these types, this text is written from a recognition that rate and comprehension interact to produce efficient and flexible readers. Reading rate, then, is approached as a variable that, along with others, must be controlled or manipulated within a particular reading situation to produce the desired results. Many students feel that a low reading rate is at the core of their reading problem, and that if only they could learn to read faster, their problems would be solved. Actually, low reading rate is more often a symptom than a problem in itself.

In explaining the balance of rate and comprehension to students it is useful to present rate and comprehension as trade-offs, much like price and quality in the purchase of consumer goods. It is useful, too, to discuss rate as a symptom of a problem, rather than a cause. Many slow readers do not realize that reading at a low rate often indicates comprehension difficulty and that they read slowly because of this. One effective way to explain this relationship is to use the analogy of a fever. A fever ordinarily suggests that something else is wrong in the body, an infection or body malfunction. The fever, then, is a symptom of a problem, but it is not the cause. Similarly, a low reading rate often suggests that the reader is experiencing some other reading difficulty. With college readers, the problem is most often literal comprehension skills. However, for a student functioning at eighth grade level or below, for example, the problem may be traced to lack of word recognition skills, phonetic analysis, or word meaning acquisition. An entire unit of the text is devoted to the development of literal comprehension skills. However, no attempt was made to include instructional units on word recognition, phonics, or core vocabulary development because a student who lacks these basic skills is not ready to handle other skills developed throughout the text.

TREATMENT OF CONCENTRATION AND RETENTION

Concentration and recall of information are two important skills that directly affect whether a student reads efficiently. For example, a student who spends several hours attempting to read a textbook chapter, but is unable to concentrate, has used his or her time inefficiently. Likewise, a student who reads at a high rate of speed but cannot recall what has been read when he or she finishes is inefficient. For this reason, a unit on recall and concentration has been included in the text. It presents practical suggestions for improving concentration and reviewing material to strengthen recall, and systems for learning while reading. The unit also discusses underlining, marginal notations, and summary notes as devices for improving long-term recall.

VOCABULARY DEVELOPMENT

A basic store of knowledge of word meanings is at the root of efficient and flexible reading. Unless a student has working knowledge and control of a vocabulary, he or she will read neither efficiently nor flexibly. Instead, a reader lacking an adequate vocabulary will read hesitantly, stumbling over or skipping unknown words. Comprehension will diminish as confusions over word meanings arise; rate will fluctuate as the reader encounters unknown words.

Because of its importance in the overall development of mature reading behaviors, vocabulary is discussed in two chapters in the text. Both chapters employ a practical approach to vocabulary development because few students have the time or desire to undertake an extensive program of word study. Practical solutions to problems such as multiple word meanings are addressed, and easily developed skills are suggested.

CRITICAL READING SKILLS

The abilities to interpret, evaluate, and apply what one reads to real-life situations are essential for an active, mature reader. A vital aspect in the development of an efficient and flexible reader, then, is acquisition of critical reading skills. Too often students and content area instructors alike assume that literal comprehension and recall (the careful, complete understanding of factual content) are all that are needed. Both often fail to recognize the need to interpret, assess, evaluate, and criticize written material. Unit Six in the text is devoted to developing several essential critical reading skills. The first chapter is concerned with interpretative skills, the second with evaluative skills.

INTERCHANGEABLE INSTRUCTIONAL UNITS

Many instructors have developed preferred instructional sequences that are particularly effective for the type of course they teach and well suited to the needs of their students. Because of this preference, the sections of this book are interchangeable rather than sequentially dependent. Instructors, then, are not limited to teaching the skills in the order in which they are presented.

READING SELECTIONS: CONTROLLED DIFFICULTY

Two reading selections follow each chapter in Units Two through Eight in the text. The difficulty of the first in each chapter is designated Difficulty Level A, the second, Difficulty Level B. Level A corresponds to a readability level in grades 8-10, whereas level B corresponds to reading grade levels 11-13. The readability of each selection was determined using the Fry Readability Graph. The Fry Graph requires three distinct 100-word passages to be selected from within the article and analyzed for sentence length and syllabic complexity. Readability research over the past several years has confirmed its reliability and validity.

The bilevel reading selections can be used in a variety of ways.

1. An instructor may use the readings to progress from simple to complex, first assigning the level A reading and, once students have experienced success, advancing them to more difficult, challenging readings.
2. An instructor may decide to individualize within a class of varying skill levels, assigning level A to some students and level B to others. Depending, of course, on the manner in which the instructor conducts the class, this approach may prove effective by assigning each student materials within his or her skill range, thus avoiding frustration and negative feedback.
3. Because the selections vary widely in content, organization, and styles, an instructor may choose the selection that is more appropriate to the interest level, major fields of study, skill deficiencies, age, or cultural level of the class.
4. Recognizing that student motivation is crucial to learning, an instructor may allow students to choose the selection they will read in each chapter. Students, no doubt, will quickly realize that selection A is easier than selection B. Some students will challenge themselves by choosing the more difficult B selections; others will recognize their limitations and need for success and choose A selections.
5. If only one selection is used to complete in-chapter assignments, then the second can be used in several ways. First, an instructor may return to unused selections at a later time for additional skill practice or reinforcement. For instance, an unused selection in one of the early chapters might be used to provide additional practice with skimming or scanning. Second, unused selections may be assigned to advanced students who seem eager for skill application. Finally, unused readings may be individually assigned to students who exhibit a specific skill deficiency and can benefit from additional guided practice.

In essence, the two levels of selections provide the instructor and the student, with flexibility and alternatives.

MULTIPLE-CHOICE QUESTIONS

The multiple-choice questions that follow each reading selection are designed to cover both literal and interpretative comprehension skills, as well as the ability to determine word meaning in context. Item 1 checks students' understanding of the main idea, 2-5 measure recall of details, 6 tests ability to determine word meaning in context, and 7-10 measure critical reading skills.

Because the multiple-choice questions are structured systematically throughout the text, they permit the student and the instructor to evaluate the error pattern and to determine areas of strengths and weakness. For example, a student who regularly misses question 1 is experiencing difficulty identifying the main ideas. Frequent errors in items 2-5 suggest lack of attention to detail. The student may be reading too fast or may not comprehend the relationship between key ideas as they support the main idea. Students who experience difficulty with item 6 need further instruction and practice in the use of contextual aids, and students who make frequent errors with items 7-10 have difficulty reading critically.

PRACTICE EXERCISES

Many students need help in applying and transferring skills. Often the mere presentation of a technique is not sufficient. Students require a number of situations in which they can experiment with, practice, and apply skills that have been presented. To help meet this need, three types of practice exercises are included in the text:

1. in-chapter exercises
2. exercises based on reading selections included in the text
3. exercises using students' own materials

The in-chapter exercises are constructed to provide immediate practice and allow the student to test a skill as it is being taught. They also give the student immediate feedback on the various techniques and skills. The exercises based on reading selections encourage students to integrate the skills taught in the chapter. In these exercises students are given the opportunity to apply techniques to materials specifically chosen to be appropriate for the skill to be applied. Thus students are guided to experience initial success with each technique. A third type of exercise allows students to apply techniques to various types of material that they are currently reading. These exercises emphasize the need to apply skills learned in the course to everyday reading situations.

PRETESTS AND POSTTESTS

The text contains pretests and posttests that provide the student and the instructor with an assessment of the student's incoming and exit skill levels as well as an indication of the amount of improvement made. Chapters 2 and 19 each contain a test that measures overall reading efficiency and a three-part test that indicates degree of reading flexibility. Each of the tests is described, details of its construction are presented, and suggestions for use and interpretation are given in the following sections.

Reading Efficiency Test

The Reading Efficiency Pretest and Posttest consist of general-interest articles taken from the same publication. Ten multiple-choice questions, structurally similar to the questions contained at the end of each reading selection, follow the articles. The articles were selected from the same publication to minimize differences in format, size of print, author's style, line length, and so forth. For each test, the student is directed to read the article, record his or her reading time, complete and score the multiple-choice questions, and compute a Reading Efficiency Score.

Reading Flexibility Tests

The Reading Flexibility Pretests and Posttests are comprised of three different subtests. Each test directs the student to read a passage for a specific purpose. The first directs the student to read an excerpt from a psychology text for the purpose of taking an exam based on its content. Ten multiple-choice questions are used to measure comprehension. The second subtest directs the student to read a magazine article to locate only the most important ideas in the article. For this subtest five open-ended questions are used to measure the student's recall of main ideas. The third test, taken from a reference book on botany, directs the student to read to find the answer to a specific question, and that question is used as the measure of comprehension following the article. You can see, then, that the first selection requires careful, close reading, the second directs the student to skim for main ideas, and the third asks the student to scan. As was done for the Reading Efficiency Test, pretests and posttests were taken from the same publication to minimize textual differences.

By comparing Reading Efficiency Scores for each of the three subtests of either the pretest or posttest, the student can obtain an indication of reading flexibility. A student who reads each of the passages in a similar way would find that the Reading Efficiency Scores are also very similar. However, for a student who reads flexibly, varying speed to suit the purpose and type of material, the Reading Efficiency Scores will vary significantly.

Pretest-Posttest Comparisons

By comparing the results of pretests with those of posttests, the student can obtain an estimate of improvement. On the Reading Efficiency Test, the student can note an increase in the RES from pretest to posttest. Similarly, for the Reading Flexibility Test, the student can observe a wider range of RESs across the three subtests between pretests and posttests. Chapter 19 contains an Evaluation Chart that enables the student to make these comparisons easily.

Chapter 2

GENERAL SUGGESTIONS FOR TEACHING THE COURSE

STRUCTURING THE COURSE

Classroom Arrangement

A comfortable, nonthreatening classroom environment is most suitable for instruction. The arrangement, however, should have enough structure to encourage students to approach the class seriously and attentively. It is useful to arrange the seating so that the instructor can readily observe each student as he or she reads.

Class Scheduling

Because regular practice, frequent repetition, and reinforcement of skills are needed, frequent class meetings are necessary. At least two class sessions per week are needed; three or four sessions per week are desirable.

Student Conferences

At the beginning of the semester, the scheduling of individual conferences is an effective way to become acquainted with each student and his or her individual needs. During the conference, you can make sure that the course is appropriate for the student and begin to identify the student's individual strengths and weaknesses. The conference is also a good opportunity to review with the student the results of any reading or achievement tests that may have been used in placing the student in or recommending him or her for the course.

Students respond extremely favorably to the opportunity to meet with the instructor individually. Students with reading problems are eager to discuss their problem with someone, and students eager to further develop their reading skills welcome the occasion to discuss their particular profile of skills.

Many instructors use the initial conference to get a verbal commitment from the student, an acknowledgment that he or she is interested in the course and plans to approach it seriously. A student who is committed to the course feels obligated to attend, participate in class, and apply the skills learned to other courses.

Periodic progress-check conferences are useful throughout the semester to help motivate the student, provide feedback on his or her progress, check on whether he or she is applying the skills taught to other materials, and encourage him or her to do so.

An end-of-the-course evaluation conference can be scheduled to review the student's work, discuss any end-of-semester tests results, and suggest areas for further study.

Attendance Policy

Regular class attendance should be emphasized. If college policy permits, an attendance requirement or maximum number of allowable absences should be established at the beginning of the course. Students seldom can develop on their own the skills presented and discussed in class. Also, many students need the direction and structure that an attendance policy provides. While discussing your attendance policy with the students, you might suggest that if they could learn to read efficiently and flexibly on their own, they would have done so already and would not need to attend class.

If college policy does not allow you to establish an attendance policy, an alternative is to structure the grading system so that regular class attendance is necessary to complete in-class assignments or take weekly quizzes or mastery tests.

Credit/Noncredit

Always an important issue in regard to any type of reading-study course is the awarding of degree credit for course completion. Although many colleges grant credit for such a course, some do not; several others award credit but do not accept it toward the fulfilling of degree requirements.

When a particular institution does not give degree credit for the course, the reason usually given is that remedial work does not deserve college credit. Students, of course, argue vehemently that they do as much work and learn as much in a reading-study course as in other courses they take. Often, the issue of credit can influence student motivation and performance. If your institution will not award credit, a strategy to use to change this policy is to offer the course as noncredit at first. Then, as the course is taught, document new skill learning that occurs and show that students are learning techniques that they were never taught previously. Also, retain records of the number of hours of student work required and the assignments given. These materials will be useful if the department decides at some point to submit the course for credit.

Grading Policy

A grading system is difficult to establish for a reading-study course. As for any other college course, there are advantages and disadvantages to most grading systems. A number of options, and their pros and cons, are summarized below.

1. Traditional Quizzes and Exams. Although these are easy to prepare and provide a fairly objective evaluation of the student's progress, usually they do measure students' ability to recall facts, principles, and techniques taught.

They do not measure whether or not the students can use the techniques to read or study better. In most courses in which skill learning is the focus, the evaluation process involves performance of the skill. (In a typing class, for instance, the student is not often evaluated on what he or she knows about typing, but rather on how fast and accurately he or she types.)

2. Skill Application Quizzes and Exams. Exams that are constructed to measure how effectively a student can perform a skill are a workable alternative to traditional quizzes. Test situations that approximate practical use situations, requiring the student to demonstrate that he or she has learned the particular skill or technique, can be devised for many skills. The skill of identifying the main idea, for instance, can be tested by asking the student to underline the main idea. Textbook underlining can be evaluated by asking the student to underline a sample textbook page.

3. The Contract System. A contract system is frequently used in skill courses where the amount of application and practice are crucial to learning. Contracts can be established with a class as a whole or with students individually.

   A class contract details the amount of work and the assignments a student must complete in order to earn a grade of A, B, or C. A sample contract plan is included on page 29 of this manual. Generally, a class contract would cover most of the skills taught in the course.

   Individual student contracts that focus on areas in which the student needs further work and additional practice can be written. A student who has difficulty identifying main ideas, for instance, will also have difficulty underlining effectively. A contract could be devised in which the student completes additional practice in identifying main ideas and further work on underlining and marking.

The individual student contract is particularly workable if a reading laboratory or library reference area that houses additional and supplementary instructional materials is available.

Student Records

Many instructors find it useful to keep a manila file folder for each student. They would keep all the student's work and assignments, tests, and grading contracts, as well as any additional handouts or worksheets distributed in class in the folder. The folders should be brought to each class session and distributed at the beginning of class. Instructors who use this system find that it is convenient to have all materials readily available to be used for reference, follow-up, or examples. If the organization of course materials is left completely to the students, instructors find that many of them come to class without the materials the instructor wishes to use.

Bringing Textbook and Content Textbook to Class

At the beginning of the semester, you will avoid much frustration if you insist that each student always bring the text to class. Also, you may want to require that students bring one other text or nonfiction paperback to class for use in skill applications.

ORGANIZING THE COURSE CONTENT

The text is structured into self-contained sections, or units, to permit flexibility in organizing course content. Depending on the type of student, the priority individual instructors place on particular skills, and the time during the semester that the course is offered, many instructors have strong preferences about what skills should be taught first and how skills should be sequenced. Instructors are encouraged to use the text as best suits their individual needs.

Specific suggestions for organizing and structuring course content are offered below.

Skill Orientation

It is important clearly to establish the course as skill-oriented and to emphasize that performance, not acquisition of knowledge, is the criterion of success. The overall goal of the course is to enable the student to become an efficient and flexible reader.

Tightly Structuring the Course

Many students enrolled in a reading course require organization and structure in order to feel comfortable. They are often confused by a loosely structured or flexible course organization in which course objectives are unclear. The following suggestions may be useful in helping students understand the organization and structure of the course.

1. Distribute a skill agenda. Before classes begin, instructors usually plan out what they will teach each week throughout the semester. Students respond well if the instructor shares the semester's plan with them. They like to know what to expect and what the course will include. A skill agenda, listing the skill(s) to be covered each week, with corresponding dates, can easily be prepared from your own plans. A sample skill agenda is included at the end of this manual.
2. Distribute course requirements and a statement of the grading system. Despite clear verbal explanations, some students do not understand or do not remember information they are given about course requirements. Students are able to organize themselves more effectively if they are given a list of assignments, due dates, test dates, and a statement of how these will be used to determine grades.
3. Relate and connect class sessions to one aother. Although a skill agenda clearly defines how the course is organized

and shows how skills relate to one another, it is useful to reinforce this organization almost daily by tying together the previous class session with the current one, and at the end of a session, giving a brief preview of the next class.

Collecting Student Data

It is useful to collect some basic information from each student during one of the first class sessions. In addition to such information as name, address, phone, and social security number, useful for general record keeping, you might ask each student to indicate the following:

1. curriculum and faculty advisor
2. year in college
3. current grade point average, if any
4. whether he or she has taken a reading course before, and if so, where and when

Each of these items will help you to become familiar with each student and to adjust your content and approach to meet the particular needs of each class.

Pretesting and Posttesting

If students have not taken a standardized reading test before entering the course, you might consider including a reading test as part of your first week's activities.

A standardized reading test, most importantly, will give you an overview of the student's incoming ability. If the test reports a grade level or grade equivalency score, the results will give you an indication of the level at which the student can function adequately and suggest types of materials appropriate to the student. Also, depending on the text used, it may indicate areas of strengths and weaknesses. To the student, the test results will demonstrate the need for the course and may motivate him or her to strive for improvement.

An alternative form of the same test at the end of the course can function as a posttest, and when compared to the pretest, can indicate the improvement a student has made. Posttests are particularly encouraging to students, because they provide clear, measurable evidence of their improvement. Although pretests and posttests are included in the text, they are intended only to provide students with an estimate of their efficiency and flexibility and not to provide an overall assessment of reading skills and deficiencies.

A selected bibliography of standardized reading tests appropriate for college students is included at the end of this manual.

Class Session Format

Since many students have relatively short attention spans and have difficulty concentrating and maintaining interest for an extended period of time, it is important to include a variety of activities within each class session. Many students would, for example, have difficulty working on identifying main ideas for an entire class session of fifty to sixty minutes. It would be more effective to divide up the time by working with main ideas for twenty to thirty minutes and then switching to a follow-up activity on a previously taught skill, such as prereading, for the remaining time.

Skill Application and Transfer

The immediate goal in any reading course is to teach students skills and techniques. Teaching these skills is fairly clear-cut; however, the long-range goal of encouraging students to apply and transfer skills they have learned to daily reading experiences is more difficult.

The skill application exercises contained in the text are written to assist instructors in skill transfer. Instructors may also find the following suggestions useful.

1. Conduct a class discussion early in the semester about the utility of the skills and the importance of using them as they are learned. You might jokingly ask students if while walking down the street they have ever been stopped by a person and asked to explain the SQ3R reading-study method, or whether they expect that situation ever to occur. This line of questioning demonstrates to the students that the skill is of no real value, except to themselves, and that it must be used in order to be valuable.
2. Make specific assignments to be completed in the student's own reading material. Although the text contains numerous skill application exercises, instructors are encouraged to make additional assignments.
3. Informally spot-check the students and observe their reading behaviors in order to determine if they are using the skills taught. For example, ask the students to turn to a chapter in one of the texts that they have just finished reading. Ask them to check whether they underlined and marked it or whether they made any marginal notes, and whether they reviewed it after they read it. Or, as you ask students to read a particular assignment, and as they begin reading, observe how many students preread the material before reading it.

Chapter 3

APPROACHES TO EACH SECTION OF THE TEXT

UNIT ONE: GETTING STARTED

The purpose of the first section of the text is to establish a framework. Specifically, the section attempts to create a base of understanding about the interrelationship among reading rate, comprehension and related variables and encourages students to develop realistic expectations about their reading rate improvement. An integral part of setting goals and expectations is an awareness of one's current level of skill. One specific purpose, accomplished by the pretests included in Chapter 2, is to provide the student with an indication of his or her current level of performance. These pretests will also be used later, along with the posttests, to compute gain and analyze improvement.

As students begin the course, it is useful for them to become familiar with the expectations, attitudes, and possible misconceptions that they may have toward reading in general, and more specifically, toward reading rate improvement. You might initiate a discussion by asking students to respond to questions such as the following: What do you expect to learn in this course? Are you a slow or fast reader? How fast is fast? Do you know anyone who can speed read? Have you heard advertisements for speed reading courses? If so, what promises do they make?

In the midst of general, preliminary discussions about the course, one student will invariably ask the instructor, "How fast do _you_ read?" This question affords the ideal opportunity to introduce the concept of reading flexibility. You can reply by asking the student whether he or she wants to know how fast you read the comic strips, a newspaper editorial, or a car loan contract, explaining that you would read each differently.

It is advisable to allow students to "settle in" to the course and to feel comfortable and confident about the course before asking them to complete the pretests. If the pretests are given too early in the course (such as the first class meeting) some students may become discouraged; others may not perform as well as they are able due to the initial anxiety and confusion of the first few days of a college semester.

Also, before attempting the pretests, students should fully understand their purpose. It is important that students understand that the pretests are not traditional quizzes or exams and will not be used to determine their grade in the course. If students think their grade will be based on improvement noted between pretest and posttest comparison, the grade-conscious student may recognize the advantage of scoring low on the pretests in order to produce significant gain on pretest-posttest comparisons.

Two effective uses of the pretest are: (1) to establish individual goals with each student and (2) to obtain a commitment from each student to work toward those goals. When motivated by a specific goal, students often work harder, take the course more seriously, and commit necessary amounts of time to practice and skill application.

UNIT TWO: HOW TO READ EFFICIENTLY

This section is intended to introduce some preliminary skills that contribute to reading efficiency. The skills taught in these two chapters were deliberately chosen because they are easy to learn and can make dramatic differences almost immediately. Personal experience, as well as learning research, has demonstrated the importance of providing positive, successful learning experiences early in an instructional program. Students do respond positively to the skills presented in this unit, especially prereading and reading in phrases.

Reading with a Purpose

Reading with a purpose is best presented as a means of focusing attention and remembering what is read. An extremely common student complaint is that they cannot remember what they read. Even students with above-average reading abilities frequently experience this problem. If the student adequately comprehends the material as he or she reads it but cannot recall it later, a common reason is that the student had not established specific purposes for reading or intentions to remember. Students usually read a chapter because it has been assigned. They do not approach the chapter with the intent to find out more about a particular topic or to relate textbook content to information already presented in the classroom lecture. And because they are looking for nothing in particular as they read, they recall little or nothing.

Usually, students are convinced easily of the value of establishing purposes for reading, particularly if it is demonstrated by using several everyday examples. You might ask the students to suggest day-to-day situations in which a purpose is established before an activity is begun. They might offer such things as knowing what you are going to buy before going shopping, setting a time or a distance goal before starting out jogging, knowing how much you want or are able to spend before going to a restaurant, or knowing what information you need before going to the library.

A more difficult task is to teach students to develop appropriate and useful questions. In fact, the most common difficulty that students experience in establishing purposes and forming questions is that of constructing questions that are specific and that relate directly to the main topics covered in the material read. Strongly discourage formation of questions that can be answered in a word or two. Students, of course, will experience greater difficulty in establishing purposes for reading material that does not employ headings. When forced to rely on the first sentence of each paragraph, students are more reluctant to take the additional reading time required. You might emphasize that reading with specific purposes is even more important when reading material that lacks the organizational and structural aids provided by the headings.

Textual Aids

A discussion of textual aids is included in the text to emphasize their importance and to illustrate their use. Basically, students need to see textual aids as devices that clarify, explain, emphasize, summarize, or organize information. Students tend to ignore some textual aids, such as pictures, graphs, and charts, and fail to make the most effective use of others, including headings and enumeration.

A useful way to demonstrate the importance of graphs, maps, charts, and pictures is to use the following activity. Refer the students to one of the graphs or charts included in the text. Allow them to study it and then ask them to write a paragraph that contains all the information contained in the graph or chart. Students will soon realize that the graph or chart is a highly concise but complicated form of expression containing a great deal of information and that to replace it with words produces repetitious, cumbersome writing.

Reading in Phrases

In presenting phrase reading, the emphasis should be on meaning rather than on speed. Students should view phrase reading as a technique that "puts words together that naturally go together" rather than as a way to read faster by reducing the number of fixations. Reading faster, then, is the end product, but facilitating comprehension is the more immediate goal.

You may find that some students experience difficulty and frustration in attempting to phrase read. Often this difficulty suggests more serious reading problems. The student may have problems with word recognition or word meaning, or poor sentence comprehension skills. On the other hand, a good reader who has trouble phrase reading is often trying too hard and, as such, is interfering with the natural flow of reading.

Prereading

Prereading is a procedure that allows a reader to become familiar with any type of material before reading it. Research has documented its value in improving reading efficiency, and its worth is further attested to by its inclusion in nearly all of the reading-study systems published in the past thirty years. The technique is built on the psychological concept of mind set, or expectancy, and its validity is well substantiated in verbal learning theory.

The technique of prereading will be new to most students, and they will be cautious at first. It is important to provide an opportunity in class for students to try the method and then to react to and ask questions about it. The quiz included in the chapter directs the students to preread a sample selection and answer some general questions about its content. As a follow-up to this exercise, and to further demonstrate the amount of information that one acquires while prereading, you might ask students what additional information (other than the answers to the exercise questions) they learned as they preread. As students respond, list the information on the chalkboard. As the list grows, students will be impressed with the amount of information that is acquired through prereading and may become convinced of its value.

The most common mistake students make in prereading is that they spend more time than is actually necessary and attempt to read too much. To prevent this problem and to shape correct prereading techniques, it is useful to set a time limit for class exercises. This will force students along and will partially answer the common objection to the technique, "It takes too long!"

The obvious challenge to the instructor is to ensure that students will transfer their skill in prereading to their daily assignments and leisure reading. Although there is no certain way to effect transfer, a cue reduction method has been successful for many instructors. This involves gradually diminishing the frequency of specific directions and reminders to preread. Right after you have taught prereading, always direct students to preread anything that you ask them to read. Then, after several weeks of constant, regular reminders, gradually phase out your reminders, so that you are giving them only occasionally. As you phase them out, observe whether students are continuing to preread before reading, without specific direction to do so. When most students preread without reminders, further reduce or eliminate the reminders. This method of gradual cue reduction is equally effective in working with many other techniques presented in the text.

UNIT THREE: HOW TO INCREASE YOUR COMPREHENSION

The comprehension skills presented in this section are the most crucial to efficient and flexible reading. A student must acquire a foundation of comprehension skills and a familiarity with the structure of sentences, paragraphs, and articles in order to begin to adjust rate to suit purpose and difficulty. The comprehension skills contained in the section are prerequisite skills for selective reading and for techniques for reading faster presented later in the text.

Reading Sentences

This chapter focuses on three sentence level skills: identifying core parts, recognizing relationships, and reading complicated sentences. Although the identification of core parts is a basic skill, many students are unable to locate readily the part of the sentence that carries the essential meaning. Identification of sentence core parts is important to literal comprehension as well as to higher level rate and flexibility skills that require selective reading. For literal comprehension, the ability to locate core parts is needed to derive the basic meaning of the sentence and to recognize and separate the parenthetical and subordinate elements of the sentence.

When students acquire sufficient skill to begin focusing on rate and flexibility, the ability to identify sentence core parts is again crucial. In skimming, for instance, in which the goal is to become familiar rapidly with the overall organization and content of a passage, the student reads selectively, reading some parts and skipping others. In sentences and paragraphs that are selected for reading, rapid identification of sentence core parts carrying the basic meaning is crucial.

The second skill presented in the chapter is recognition of sentence patterns and the relationships they suggest. Many students misread or misinterpret or do not fully comprehend sentences because they do not recognize that a sentence, by its structure, provides clues about the relationship and relative importance of the ideas it expresses.

Techniques for unraveling complicated sentences is the third skill discussed. Using previously taught skills, students are guided through a procedure that "strips away" nonessential sentence parts until the core sentence is identified.

Recognizing Paragraph Structure

A common reading problem exhibited by college students is that they do not perceive a paragraph as a separate, distinct unit of meaning. Rather, a paragraph is thought of as a string, or group, of sentences or one of many parts or pieces of a larger passage or selection. Students fail to recognize the overall organization or structure of paragraphs and do not look for the topic, main ideas, and supporting details as they read. The purpose of this chapter is to focus the students' attention on the structure of the paragraph and to provide a foundation of training and practice in identifying the key elements of a paragraph.

A student's own writing often clearly reflects his or her understanding of paragraph structure. It may be useful to collect a writing sample from the class before beginning this chapter. The samples will indicate how students perceive paragraph structure and what elements they regard as necessary. You may wish to do a quick tally, counting how many student samples had a unified topic, how many contained a clear statement of the main idea, and how many used sufficient supporting details. Then, as you begin this chapter, to demonstrate and emphasize the need to learn paragraph elements, share the results of your tally with the class.

To maintain student interest, it is helpful to foreshadow skills that you will teach later in the course that require knowledge of paragraph structure. Students' motivational level and mind set seem to improve when they understand that skimming is a technique that requires rapid location of the main idea, and this chapter teaches the concept of main idea so that they will be successful with skimming later in the course.

An additional practice exercise for emphasizing the relationship among the sentence parts and demonstrating their interdependence is to use the sentence strip method. Select a paragraph and cut it up, so that each sentence is on a separate strip of paper.

Scramble the strips and ask the students to rearrange them so that they form an organized paragraph.

To provide further practice in the recognition of supporting details, select two or three paragraphs that contain a clearly stated main idea on a closely related subject. Then, scramble the sentences that contain the supporting details. Ask the students to match each detail with the main idea it supports.

Organizational Patterns

Recognition of organizational patterns is also a vital skill for later selective reading and speed techniques. If a student is able to recognize the pattern of thought, he or she will be able to anticipate what will follow and make a judgment about its relative importance. A useful activity to demonstrate anticipation skills is to present the student with only the first two sentences of a paragraph in which the pattern is clearly suggested. Ask the students to predict what will be contained in the remainder of the paragraph.

Articles and Longer Selections

Students frequently do not realize that paragraphs, as parts of a larger piece of writing, must relate to one another. As students read, they do not connect one paragraph with another and do not look for the overall organization and structure of the passage. As a result, their passage level comprehension is limited and incomplete. The purpose of this chapter is to present skill instruction and practice in reading connected prose.

Comprehension of articles and selections is, of course, completely dependent on adequate sentence and paragraph comprehension skills, and students should not begin this chapter until they have demonstrated competency with these prerequisite skills. Because the chapter frequently draws a parallel between paragraph and passage organization, it is particularly important that students have developed skills in paragraph reading.

If a student is experiencing difficulty with lengthy material, it may be useful to approach it paragraph by paragraph. First, identify the topic and main idea of each paragraph, and then summarize what each paragraph contributes to the overall meaning of the passage. Then, tie together the meaning of each paragraph to obtain the meaning of the passage. Encourage students to use this approach whenever they have difficulty understanding a passage.

For students experiencing difficulty in identifying the thesis statement, it may be useful to reduce the article to a skeletal outline, containing only main ideas from each of the paragraphs. Elimination of the details makes it easier for students to see the relationship of ideas.

When teaching this topic, it is again important to begin to make preliminary connections between skills taught in this chapter and their use in later techniques. Although these skills are valuable and important in themselves, students become more interested if they realize they are the foundation for later "speed" techniques.

UNIT FOUR: HOW TO REMEMBER WHAT YOU READ

At this point it is necessary to make the distinction between comprehension and retention. Whereas comprehension refers to understanding of printed material while reading, retention refers to recall of material at a delayed time period after reading. An efficient reader, to accomplish long-range as well as immediate goals, must achieve both comprehension and retention. For instance, a student who reads a textbook chapter in preparation for an exam must understand the material as he or she reads, as well as recall the information at a later time. The overall purpose of this section is to provide techniques and suggestions for insuring long-term recall. As a starting point, the section discusses concentration, a prerequisite for any type of recall. Then the importance of review is considered as well as various aids and systems for remembering what is read. Finally, various notetaking and marking systems are discussed.

Reading-Study Systems

Reading-study systems, the result of combining the reading process with principles of learning, are step-by-step methods of learning while reading. Although there is substantial research evidence that reading-study systems are effective, students are often reluctant to use them. One of the most important goals for the instructor to establish in presenting this chapter is to present it convincingly.

Occasionally, some actual hands-on proof is useful in convincing students that reading-study systems are valuable and worthwhile. You might conduct an informal experiment that will demonstrate the effectiveness of the SQ3R study system. If the class is large enough, divide it into two groups (for smaller classes of which you teach multiple sections, designate one class section as Group 1, and another section as Group 2). Select a traditional textbook passage of about two to three pages for the students to read, and prepare a set of multiple-choice questions based on it. As you present the passage, vary the instructions for each group. Ask one group to read the passage only once and then answer the questions. Instruct the second group to apply the SQ3R method as they read and then to complete the questions. Then score the multiple-choice questions for each group and compute the average score for each. The group that used the SQ3R method most likely will have a higher score. Share these results with the class, and ask students from the higher scoring group why they think they did better. In order for this experiment to work for a class containing a small number of students, try to balance the groups, in terms of general ability level and numbers of severely deficient readers. Also, be sure that the passage you select is not so difficult that most of the students will be unable to read it. Students are more convinced of the utility of SQ3R if they realize that they are already familiar with some of the steps in the method. Point out that the S and Q steps of SQ3R are really prereading and establishing a purpose and that they have already learned these skills in Unit Two (Chapters 3 and 4) of the text--"How to Read Efficiently."

A common objection students raise about the SQ3R system is that it takes too long. You need to help them realize that using a reading-study method does not require any more time than they currently spend in reading a chapter at one time and then studying it later. In the SQ3R system, reading and studying are combined, and using SQ3R involves only a reallocation of time.

Because students are often skeptical about adopting a completely new way of reading and studying, it is important that their first experience with the method be a positive one. To ensure that their first attempt is reasonably successful, it is advisable to have the students first use the method in class, where they can ask questions and you can observe their work. Try to identify those students who seem confused and are not using the method properly, and offer individual help as needed.

Underlining and Marking

The most important thing students should realize about textbook marking is that it eliminates the need to reread everything in order to review and study the material. Students must recognize underlining and marking as a vital step in the review process.

To some students, the idea of underlining and marking is completely new. In most high schools, where texts and references are owned by the school district and loaned to students, textbook marking is not permitted. As a result, few students have had any experience in doing this, and they require very specific instructions on how to begin.

The most common problem students experience in underlining is underlining too much. This partially results from the attitude that "if it's in print it must be important and I have to learn it." The tendency to underline too much may, in some cases, also indicate a comprehension problem. A student who underlines nearly everything may not be able to recognize the important details that support the main idea; or he or she may have difficulty understanding the main idea and therefore may not know which details support it.

A student who underlines too little may be having difficulty understanding the passage. For such a student, check to see what he or she is underlining. If the main idea of the paragraph is not underlined and he or she has marked only a few of the details, you can be fairly certain that a comprehension problem is interfering with the ability to underline.

If a serious comprehension deficiency is blocking a student's progress, it may be necessary to teach underlining skills using easy-to-read material. For students with adequate comprehension skills who are having difficulty underlining, it is important to be certain that they can recognize too much and too little underlining. When students can recognize flawed underlining, they have demonstrated that they understand the concept of effective underlining and are ready to begin reading and underlining.

If a student continues to experience difficulty in underlining, it is sometimes useful to stop working with passages or textbook sections and focus on single paragraphs. A very basic, insecure student or a very slow reader is often overwhelmed by the task of reading and underlining several pages. After the student masters single paragraphs, move gradually toward longer passages, first using a passage comprised of two very brief paragraphs and gradually increasing the length.

As students develop the basic concept of effective underlining and the gross problems of too much or too little underlining are solved, more subtle problems arise. The system of underlining may lack consistency; the underlining may not reflect accurately the content or organization of the passage; or the underlining, although effective at the time, may not be suited for review purposes. Each of these problems are addressed in the chapter and are accompanied by illustrations and/or practice exercises.

A class activity for additional underlining practice that students particularly enjoy is underlining a passage and then trading papers and evaluating one another's underlining. Another activity is to form groups and ask each to select the best example of underlining from among the work of group members.

When a student has mastered underlining, then it is appropriate for the topic of textbook marking to be discussed. Marking is done when underlining alone does not convey the ideas adequately, show the relative importance of ideas, or indicate relationships among facts and ideas. Thus, a student must be able to underline effectively in order to be able to determine if marking is needed.

Students with weak comprehension skills may experience difficulty writing summary notes. Constructing a summary note not only requires that the student be able to understand each paragraph and recognize the topic, main ideas, and details, but that he or she also be able to condense or summarize the paragraph content. If students are having difficulty in constructing summary notes, try to show them that a summary note is similar to the topic of the paragraph: it is one or two words that tell what the paragraph is about and that may also relate to the content of other paragraphs within the passage.

UNIT FIVE: HOW TO DEVELOP YOUR WORD EFFICIENCY

Within the reading process, vocabulary is a component skill that contributes to the desired end result--comprehension. Knowledge of individual word meaning is, of course, essential in order to gain meaning from larger units of sentences, paragraphs, and passages.

Although the vocabulary of many college students is not extensive, it is seldom the primary cause of poor reading skill. Instead, a limited vocabulary is an effect of limited amounts of reading and the necessity, while reading, to struggle to comprehend the larger meaning instead of focusing on individual words.

One purpose of this unit is to provide specific techniques that students can use to expand their vocabulary. Vocabulary is often regarded by students as a dull, even boring, topic and is classified, along with spelling, as a routine task that requires rote memorization. The techniques included in this section are those which are most practical and produce fairly immediate results. College students seldom have the ambition or motivation to undertake an in-depth program of vocabulary development. They are interested, however, in effective methods of vocabulary development that they can use as they read their college texts.

A second purpose of the unit is to develop an awareness of the complexities of word meaning that provide the base for critical reading skills. Students must be familiar with denotative and connotative meanings, for example, before they can work with skills such as making inferences, determining author's purpose, and so forth.

Technical and Specialized Vocabulary

An important factor in the mastery of any subject area is the ability to learn and use the terminology that is specific to that academic area. Knowledge and control of the language of a subject area enables the student to understand textbooks and class lectures more accurately and completely, to communicate effectively in class discussions, and to demonstrate his or her mastery of the subject matter on tests and examinations.

During the first semester, most college students enroll in several courses with which they have little or no previous experiences. Courses in the social sciences, for example, each represent a new discipline to which students have had little introduction; many students have no idea what subject matter is studied in sociology or anthropology.

At first, students are confused and even overwhelmed by the unfamiliar and seemingly complicated language used by the textbook and by their instructor. It may be useful to discuss with students the need for and value of specific terminology, or jargon, within a subject area. Often, students do not realize that technical vocabulary contributes to the precision, clarity, and accuracy of the communication process in that subject area. Instead, students sometimes regard the use of specialized terminology as "using big words" or "showing off."

To demonstrate the efficiency and expediency of using specialized terminology rather than everyday words, you might select a textbook passage and present two versions of it to the class. For the first version, identify each specialized term and replace it with its definition, as taken from the text's glossary. The second version will be much longer and more complicated, by virtue of the inclusion of the definition. Ask the students to read both versions and discuss which is easier to read. Students will quickly realize the need for a single, specialized term.

To further demonstrate that specialized vocabulary contributes to language precision and eliminates confusion, you might use a sentence that contains several words that have multiple meanings. First, read or write the original sentence for the class. Then, substitute an alternative but inappropriate meaning for the word and present it again. Of course the sentence will not make sense, because the precise word meaning was not used in the second sentence. Students will readily see that everyday language can result in confusion and misinterpretation and will recognize the need for a word that has a specific, specialized meaning.

Using Contextual Aids

A student's first reaction, on meeting a word he or she does not know, is often to skip over it and continue reading. Although students know they shouldn't do this, they think their only alternative is to look the word up in the dictionary. Many students do not realize that there is an alternative to the dictionary. Specifically, they are not aware that, often, the meaning of a word can be determined by an analysis of its context.

Students can easily understand the use of context in determining word meaning, if its use is first demonstrated using spoken examples. You might dictate a sentence in which one word is missing, and then ask the students to guess the missing word. Next, give the class a sentence in which one word has been translated into French or German. Dictate the sentence and ask the class to give the English translation of the foreign word. Finally, present a sentence in which an unfamiliar English word appears and follow the same procedure, asking the students to give a synonym for the unknown word. This procedure demonstrates to a student that the context of a word often provides a clue to its meaning.

An interesting class activity using context clues involves asking each student to identify five difficult or unfamiliar words from an instructor's lecture or from one of his or her textbooks. Then, direct each student to write one sentence for each word in which the meaning of the word can be determined from analysis of the context. Have the students exchange papers and use the context to determine the meaning and write a synonym for each word.

In teaching the use of context, it is important to emphasize that context clues are not always useful in determining word meaning. In some situations, the context offers no clues, and the word meaning must be checked in the glossary or dictionary. Also, emphasize to students that context clues seldom give a precise meaning of the word. In textbook reading situations in which the exact meaning is needed, the student should check the dictionary.

UNIT SIX: HOW TO INTERPRET AND EVALUATE WHAT YOU READ

Although it is essential that students strengthen and maintain literal comprehension skills, it is also important that they develop critical reading skills. Critical reading is concerned with interpreting, reacting to, evaluating, and applying what is read. As such it involves many component skills. Space does not permit coverage of each skill; instead several of the most important and immediately usable have been selected. A prerequisite skill, of course, is literal comprehension in which the reader understands the stated, surface meaning.

Critical reading involves complex and interrelated skills, many of which depend on reasoning and logical thinking. As a result, critical reading is often a complicated area of instruction in which a "readiness factor" seems to operate. Some students seem ready and eager to analyze what they read; others regard it as still another step in the spectrum of skills they must develop. One effective way to interest students in critical reading is to use higher-interest, current practice material. You might select material on a controversial topic from current magazines, paperbacks, or local or student newspapers. Then, analyze the material with the students, interpreting and evaluating the author's message. Another excellent source of introductory material is printed advertisements. Ads often involve inferences, assumptions, bias, and unstated messages.

Making Inferences

An excellent way to introduce the topic of inferences and ease students into making them readily is through the use of pictures. Select a magazine or newspaper photograph that expresses action or emotion. Ask the students to describe what is happening or how the person feels. To respond to your question the students must make inferences or "read into" the picture. Then, by asking the students how or why they responded as they did, you can lead directly into a discussion of inference.

Evaluative Reading

Students' own writing can be used effectively in teaching evaluative reading. You might begin by asking the students to write a brief essay on a particular controversial issue. It is best to choose an issue, rather than to allow students to write about an issue of their choice because students frequently waste valuable time trying to find an issue that interests them. Ask the students to define the issue and defend their position. After they have written their essays, ask them to exchange papers (or you might collect and randomly redistribute the papers) and evaluate each other's papers using the criteria outlined in Chapter 14.

UNIT SEVEN: HOW TO READ SELECTIVELY

Throughout their educational experience, the importance of the printed word has been impressed on students. As a result, many students have come to believe that if something is in print, it must be important, and since everything is important, nothing can be skipped. The first step, then, in developing selective reading skills is to dispel this notion. You might begin by demonstrating to students that not all words and sentences in a passage are equally important. First, present a sentence in which one or two connective words have been deleted. Ask the students to paraphrase the sentence or discuss the sentence's meaning and then to guess which word(s) were deleted. Then, follow the same technique with a paragraph, deleting phrases or clauses. Next, delete an entire sentence. Students will realize that basic meaning can be retained when certain parts are skipped.

A second classroom activity that is equally effective in demonstrating that reading every word is not always necessary is based on the telegram technique. Ask the students to write a simple narrative paragraph on a particular topic, such as what they did last evening. After they have finished, tell them to imagine the following situation: They must communicate a message, but every word costs them $5.00, and, of course, they want to spend as little money as possible on this assignment. They should delete from their paragraphs every word possible but still retain the basic meaning. Then, ask students to exchange papers and read each other's. Students will be able to understand the message, even though a substantial number of words have been deleted. This activity will again demonstrate that reading every word is not always necessary in order to grasp the meaning.

In discussing skimming, it is important to emphasize that skimming is not always appropriate or effective and that much depends on the purpose for reading and the type of material being read. Specifically, students should be warned that skimming is not useful for most types of textbook reading and that they should try out this technique on other types of materials.

Teaching Skimming

Skimming is a skill that directly depends on a clear understanding of the structure of sentences, paragraphs, passages, and articles and chapters. Unless students are familiar with the overall organization and structure of these units of written prose, they will be unable easily to distinguish important from unimportant information or readily to locate main ideas. Students who experience difficulty with Unit Three: How to Increase Your Comprehension, then, will most likely achieve minimal success with skimming.

Students often are confused about the difference between prereading and skimming. It is important to emphasize that prereading is one form of skimming, and it differs from the other types according to purpose. If many students seem confused, then it may be useful to briefly demonstrate each type in succession.

Teaching Scanning

An easy way to introduce students to the technique of scanning is to present it as a skill they have been using since an early age, but also as a skill that few people do effectively. You might mention several everyday situations in which scanning is appropriate; then ask students to think of others. To emphasize that most people do not scan effectively, you might dramatize everyday situations in which an easy task is not handled effectively: a sales clerk who takes "forever" to look up credit card numbers in a booklet, a salesman who cannot locate prices in a catalog, or a stock clerk attempting to locate a particular item on a grocery store shelf for a price check. In teaching scanning, it is most important to emphasize that scanning must be systematic, following a general pattern or approach. This point might be demonstrated by first allowing students to scan randomly, reading every fifth line, or some other portion, and then directing them to scan systematically using the procedure suggested in Chapter 15.

UNIT EIGHT: HOW TO INCREASE YOUR RATE AND BUILD FLEXIBILITY

This section has three purposes. First, it is designed to present three techniques for increasing reading speed. Pacing, key word reading, and rereading are each explained and guidelines provided for their use. Students should realize that these techniques are appropriate only under specific circumstances, and do not apply to all reading situations.

The second purpose of this section is to draw together many of the concepts and skills presented throughout the text into final statements about the nature of reading efficiency and flexibility. It is at this point that the student should come to an understanding (if he or she has not already) about the interaction among rate, comprehension, purpose, material, and reading technique.

A final purpose is to provide the student with an estimate of his or her present level of reading efficiency and flexibility using the posttests contained in Chapter 19. By comparing their results with the pretests, students can compare entry- and exit-level skills and assess their improvement.

Appendix

USEFUL INSTRUCTIONAL AIDS

The following instructional aids are included as examples of materials that can be developed to organize and structure the course. A sample skill agenda, a sample class contract grading sheet, and a beginning of the course data sheet are included.

Sample Skill Instruction Agenda

Week	Topic(s)	Chapter Reference
1	Course Introduction, Pretesting The Reading Process	1,2
2	Techniques for Reading Efficiency	3,4
3	Comprehension: Sentences	5
4	Comprehension: Main Ideas	6
5	Comprehension: Details, Directional Words	6
6	Comprehension: Organizational Patterns	7
7	Comprehension: Articles	8
8	Remembering What You Read	9,10
9	Vocabulary Development	11,12
10	Critical Reading Interpretation	13
11	Critical Reading: Evaluation	14
12	Skimming	15
13	Skimming	15
14	Scanning, Technique for Faster Reading	16,17
15	Reading Flexibility, Posttesting, and Evaluation	18,19

Sample Class Contract Grading Sheet

Name ______________ Instructor ______________

Semester ______________

Contract for B Grade

If you want to earn a final grade of B in the course, complete all of the following assignments. After you complete each assignment, please show your work to me. We will discuss and evaluate the effectiveness of each technique. Please keep all work in your folder. NOTE: These assignments may not be completed during class time.

Date Completed

1. Skill: Identifying Sentence Core Parts

   Assignment: Choose a 3-page selection from one of your textbooks. Read the assignment and then for each sentence, underline the core parts (only the subject and predicate). ______________

2. Skill: Identifying Topics and Main Ideas in Paragraphs

   Assignment: Choose a 5-page selection from one of your textbooks. Read the assignment and then for each paragraph, place a bracket around the topic of the paragraph and underline the main idea. ______________

3. Skill: Identifying Paragraph Organizational Patterns

   Assignment: Choose a 5-page selection from one of your textbooks. Read the assignment and for each paragraph, identify the paragraph organizational pattern and write it in the margin. ______________

4. Skill: Phrase Reading

   Assignment: Choose any two articles (2-3 pages each) of interest from any magazine or periodical. Phrase read each article and compute your WPM (estimate the number of words in the article). After you have read each article, write a brief summary of it. ______________

Date Completed

5. Skill: Textbook Underlining

   Assignment: Underline and mark a 3-page selection from one of your textbooks. Use specific techniques suggested in your text. __________

6. Skill: Key Word Reading

   Assignment: Choose any two articles (2-3 pages each) of interest from any magazine, journal, or periodical. Use key word reading for each article. After you have read each article, record the title of the article and the course. Then write a one-paragraph summary of the article. __________

7. Skill: Skimming

   Assignment: Select a paperback nonfiction, general audience book. Let me know what it is before you begin; then skim read the book. Time limit: 40 minutes. When you have finished, bring the book in during a lab session and discuss it with me. (Counts as two assignments.) __________

8. Skill: Skimming

   Assignment: Select three 3-page magazine articles. Skim each one. Spend no more than three to five minutes on each article. Record the title and source of each and write a two- to three- sentence summary of each. __________

Sample Student Data Sheet

Name: ______________________ Course: ______________________

Address: ______________________ Instructor: ______________________

Phone: ______________________ Semester: ______________________

Soc. Sec. No.: ______________________

Curriculum: ______________________

Faculty Advisor: ______________________

Semester: 1 2 3 4 5 6 (circle one)

Courses Registered for this Semester:

1. ______________________

2. ______________________

3. ______________________

4. ______________________

5. ______________________

6. ______________________

Describe any other reading courses you have taken in the past several years.

____

____

____

Why are you taking this course?

____

____

____

____

For instructor use:

Standardized Test Scores:

BIBLIOGRAPHY

MATERIALS BIBLIOGRAPHY

TESTS

California Study Methods Survey. Los Angeles, CA: California Test Bureau, 1958.
Measures school attitudes, study mechanics, and planning.

Iowa Silent Reading Test. New York, NY: Harcourt Brace Jovanovich, 1973.
Level 2 (grades 9 through 14) measures vocabulary, reading comprehension, directed reading, and reading efficiency. Level 3 (grades 11 through 16) measures vocabulary, reading comprehension, and reading efficiency.

Nelson-Denny Reading Test. Boston, MA: Houghton Mifflin, 1973, 1981.
Measures vocabulary, comprehension, and rate for grades 7 through college.

Reading Versatility Tests

Stanford Diagnostic Reading Test. New York, NY: Harcourt Brace Jovanovich, 1976.
Level 3 (grades 9 through 13) measures comprehension, word meaning, word parts, phonetic analysis, structural analysis, and rate.

Woodcock Mastery Test. Circle Pines, MN: American Guidance Service, 1973.
Letter identification, word identification, word attack, sentence comprehension, and passage comprehension for grades K through 12.

EFFICIENCY AND FLEXIBILITY

Adams, W. Royce. Developing Reading Versatility, 3rd ed. New York, NY: Holt, Rinehart and Winston, 1981.

Fry, Edward B. Reading Drills for Speed and Comprehension. Providence, RI: Jamestown Publishers, 1975.

_____. Skimming and Scanning. Providence, RI: Jamestown Publishers, 1978.

Hess, Karen M., et al. Developing Reading Efficiency. New York, NY: John Wiley and Sons, 1975.

Maxwell, Martha. Skimming and Scanning. New York, NY: McGraw-Hill, 1969.

Raygor, Alton L., and Schick, George B. Reading at Efficient Rates. New York, NY: McGraw-Hill, 1970.

Phillips, Anne D., and Sotiriou, Peter E. Steps to Reading Proficiency. Belmont, CA: Wadsworth, 1982.

Laughter, Mabel Y. Speed Reading. Columbus, OH: Charles E. Merrill, 1982.

COMPREHENSION SKILLS

Adams, W. Royce, and Spira, Jane B. Reading Beyond Words. New York, NY: Holt, Rinehart and Winston, 1978.

Flemming, Loraine, and Currie, Sara R. Reading for Results. Boston, MA: Houghton Mifflin, 1978.

Gedamke, Rudy, and Kropp, Niel. Reading as Thinking: Paragraph Comprehension. Woodcliffe Lake, NJ: Curriculum Associates, 1970.

Giroux, James, and Williston, Glenn R. Retaining Concepts and Organizing Facts. Providence, RI: Jamestown Publishers, 1974.

_____. Understanding the Main Idea. Providence, RI: Jamestown Publishers, 1974.

Glock, Marvin D., Bender, David S., Faith, Valerie, and Tosi, Karen. PROBE TWO. Columbus, OH: Charles E. Merrill, 1978.

Joffe, Irwin L. Finding Main Ideas. Belmont, CA: Wadsworth, 1970.

_____. Locating Specific Information. Belmont, CA: Wadsworth, 1971.

Kolzow, Lee, and Lehmann, Jane. College Reading: Strategies for Success. Englewood Cliffs, NJ: Prentice-Hall, 1982.

Maker, Janet, and Lenier, Minnette. College Reading. Belmont, CA: Wadsworth, 1982.

Niles, Olive, et al. Reading Tactics Series. Glenview, IL: Scott, Foresman, 1977.
Workbooks providing skill instruction in vocabulary, literal comprehension, critical skills, and rate and flexibility.

Pauk, Walter. Essential Skill Series. Providence, RI: Jamestown Publishers, 1976.
Contains practice passages at specific grade levels (3 through 12) for developing six categories of comprehension.

_____. Six-Way Paragraphs. Providence, RI: Jamestown Publishers, 1974.
Contains 100 passages for developing six essential categories of comprehension for grades 6 through college.

_____. Using the Signal Words. Providence, RI: Jamestown Publishers, 1975.
Contains brief skill instruction, with 100 practice passages chosen from literary works.

Robinson, H. Alan, et al. Strategies for Reading--Long Selections. Boston, MA: Allyn and Bacon, 1978.
Instruction followed by easy-to-read practice exercises on passage comprehension.

_____. Strategies for Reading--Paragraphs. Boston, MA: Allyn and Bacon, 1978.
Instruction followed by easy-to-read practice exercises on paragraph reading skills.

_____. Strategies for Reading--Sentences. Boston, MA: Allyn and Bacon, 1978.
Instruction followed by easy-to-read practice exercises on sentence comprehension.

Spargo, Edward, ed. Topics for the Restless. Providence, RI: Jamestown Publishers, 1974.
Discusses comprehension, vocabulary, word meaning, phonics, and study skills.

_____, and Harris, Raymond. Reading in Content Fields: English, Social Studies, Science. Providence, RI: Jamestown Publishers, 1978.
Discusses comprehension skill and gives instruction specific to particular subject fields.

_____, and Williston, Glenn. Timed Readings, Levels 1-8. Providence, RI: Jamestown Publishers, 1975.
Each Level (grades 6 through 12) consists of fifty 400-word passages for building comprehension and rate.

VOCABULARY

Brown, James I. Programmed Vocabulary. Englewood Cliffs, NJ: Prentice-Hall.

Davis, Nancy B. Vocabulary Improvement, 2nd ed. New York, NY: McGraw-Hill, 1978.

Henley, Elton F. Words for Reading. Englewood Cliffs, NJ: Prentice-Hall, 1980.

Licklider, Patricia. Building a College Vocabulary. Boston, MA: Little, Brown, 1981.

Pauk, Walter. Vocabulary in Context. Providence, RI: Jamestown Publishers, 1975.

Romaine, Jack S. Vocabulary for Adults. New York, NY: John Wiley and Sons, 1975.

Scruggs, Atwell. Steps to a Better Vocabulary, 2nd ed. Dubuque, IA: Kendall/Hunt, 1976.

Shepard, James F. College Vocabulary Skills. Boston, MA: Houghton Mifflin, 1979.

Smith, Elliott. Contemporary Vocabulary. New York, NY: St. Martin's Press, 1979.

PROFESSIONAL BIBLIOGRAPHY

Ahrendt, K. Community College Reading Programs. Newark, DE: International Reading Association, 1975.

Dechant, Emerald V., and Smith, Henry P. Psychology in Teaching Reading, 2nd ed. Englewood Cliffs, NJ: Prentice-Hall, 1977.

Herber, Harold. Teaching Reading in the Content Areas. Englewood Cliffs, NJ: Prentice-Hall, 1978.

Hill, Walter. Secondary School Reading: Process, Program, Procedure. Boston, MA: Allyn and Bacon, 1979.

Kersteins, Gene. Junior-Community College Reading/Study Skills: An Annotated Bibliography. Newark, DE: International Reading Association, 1971.

Maxwell, Martha. Improving Student Learning Skills. San Francisco, CA: Jossey-Bass, 1979.

Robinson, Francis P. Effective Reading, 4th ed. New York, NY: Harper and Row, 1970.

Little, Brown and Company
Boston

ISBN 0-316-56407-9